The Everyday Cooking Collection — W9-BHF-716

DESSERTS AND
CHOCOLATE

Licensed and produced by:

DIRECT SOURCE
SPECIAL PRODUCTS INC.

©℗1999 DIRECT SOURCE SPECIAL PRODUCTS INC.
Canada: P.O. Box 361,
Victoria Station, Westmount,
Quebec, Canada
H3Z 2V8
U.S.: P.O. Box 2189,
609 New York Road, Plattsburgh,
New York, 12903

Recipes and photos courtesy of:
Les Éditions Multi-Concept Inc.

Printed in Canada

ISBN# 1-896306-46-2

MOUSSES AND SOUFFLÉS 6

PASTRIES 18

CAKES 26

FRUITY DESSERTS 50

PIES AND TARTS 64

CRÊPES AND WAFFLES 84

PUDDINGS 90

YOGURT AND RASPBERRY MOUSSE

8 SERVINGS

Preparation Time: 35 minutes

Refrigeration Time: 2-3 hours

2 pkgs	(8g) unflavored gelatin
3/4 cup	(175 ml) fruit purée (store bought)
2/3 cup	(150 ml) raspberry yogurt
1/4 cup	(50 ml) sugar
1 cup	(250 ml) 35% cream, lightly whipped
1	sponge cake
	hot maple syrup, in sufficient quantity

RASPBERRY TOPPING

1/2 cup	(125 ml) raspberry purée
1/4 cup	(50 ml) sugar
1 pkg	(4g) gelatin, let stand in 2 tbsp (25 ml) cold water and dilute in 1/4 cup (50 ml) hot water

In a small bowl, stir together the cold water and gelatin, let stand until the gelatin softens.

In a double boiler, heat the fruit purée. Remove from the heat and add the gelatin; let cool.

Incorporate the fruit purée with the yogurt. Add the sugar and let set for 5 to 10 minutes in the refrigerator.

With a spatula, gently mix together the whipped cream and yogurt mixture.

Place the sponge cake on the bottom of a cake mold and cover with hot maple syrup. Pour the yogurt mixture onto the cake and place it in the refrigerator for 2 to 3 hours.

RASPBERRY TOPPING

In a saucepan, bring the raspberry purée and sugar to a boil. Remove from the heat and add the gelatin. Mix well and let cool.

Pour this over the yogurt and raspberry mousse and refrigerate.

HAZELNUT COFFEE MOUSSE

4 TO 6 SERVINGS
Preparation Time: 30 minutes
Cooking Time: 15 minutes

1 cup	(250 ml) 35% cream
2 tbsp	(25 ml) instant coffee granules
1/2 cup	(125 ml) ground hazelnuts
2 tsp	(10 ml) unflavored gelatin
2 tsp	(10 ml) cold water
2	egg yolks
1/2 cup	(125 ml) sugar
1 tsp	(5 ml) vanilla extract

GARNISH
whipped cream
whole hazelnuts

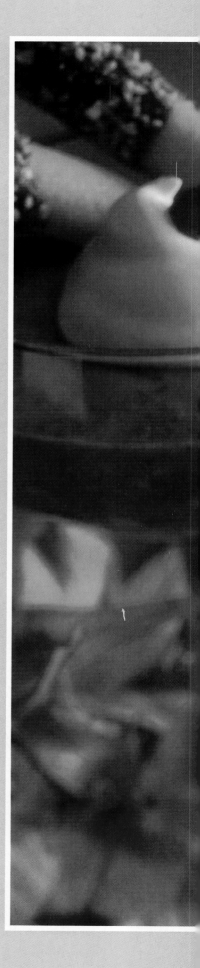

In a small double boiler, heat the cream, coffee, and hazelnuts until it reaches the boiling point. Sprinkle the gelatin in 2 tsp (10 ml) of cold water, let stand and add it to the cream mixture.

In a bowl, mix together half of the sugar, the egg yolks and hot cream. Pour into a saucepan and cook until the mixture thickens and sticks to the back of a spoon. Let cool in the refrigerator until lightly firm.

In another bowl, add the remaining sugar to the egg whites and whip to form soft peaks. Take the cream out of the refrigerator and add the vanilla, stirring constantly. Mix the two preparations together and pour into dessert cups.

Garnish with a dab of whipped cream and hazelnuts.

CRAZY CHOCOLATE MOUSSE

4 SERVINGS

Preparation Time: 10 minutes
Cooking Time: 5 minutes

2	medium eggs
2 tbsp	(25 ml) powdered cocoa
1/2 lb	(250 g) semi-sweet chocolate, melted
1/2 cup	(125 ml) 35% cream, whipped

GARNISH
    chocolate shavings

With a whisk, or an electric mixer, beat together the eggs, cocoa powder, and melted chocolate. Let cool in the refrigerator for 5 minutes.

Add the whipped cream, and mix with a wooden spoon, or spatula. Refrigerate for 15 to 20 minutes.

Use a pastry bag to fill 4 dessert cups with the chocolate mixture and garnish with the chocolate shavings.

FROZEN STRAWBERRY SOUFFLÉ

6 SERVINGS

Preparation Time: 20 minutes
Freezing Time: 4 hours

3/4 cup	(175 ml) maple syrup
1/4 cup	(50 ml) water
3/4 cup	(175 ml) strawberries
2	egg yolks
1/4 cup	(50ml) sugar
2	egg whites
1 cup	(250 ml) 35% cream

GARNISH
    strawberries

In a saucepan, bring the maple syrup, water and strawberries to a boil. Let simmer over low heat until the strawberries have softened. Purée in a food processor and set aside.

In a bowl, beat together the egg yolks and the sugar until the mixture whitens. Incorporate half of the strawberry purée and set aside.

In another bowl, whip the egg whites to form soft peaks. Slowly pour in the remaining, boiling strawberry purée, while mixing with an electric mixer.

In another bowl, whip the cream until it becomes firm. Add the other two preparations and mix gently with a spatula. Pour the mixture into ramekins and place in the freezer for at least 4 hours.

When ready to serve, remove from the molds and garnish with strawberries.

MAPLE AND CHOCOLATE SOUFFLÉ

6-8 SERVINGS
Preparation Time: 20 minutes
Freezing Time: 4 hours

2	medium egg yolks
1/4 cup	(50 ml) sugar
1/2 cup	(125 ml) maple syrup
2	medium egg whites
3/4 cup	(175 ml) 35% cream
4 oz	(125 g) semi-sweet chocolate, melted
2 tsp	(10 ml) cocoa powder

In a bowl, beat together the egg yolks and sugar until the mixture whitens. Incorporate half of the maple syrup and set aside.

In a small saucepan, bring the other half of the maple syrup to a boil and keep hot. In another bowl, beat the egg whites to form soft peaks. Slowly pour the hot maple syrup into the beaten egg whites, stirring continuously until the mixture cools. Set aside.

In a bowl, whip the cream until it becomes firm (reserve a small portion of whipped cream for garnishing). Add the other two preparations to the bowl, and mix delicately.

Cut strips of wax paper and tape them to the topsides of 6 to 8 ramekins.

Pour the mixture into the ramekins, filling them 1/4 in (1/2 cm) from the top of the wax paper. Place the ramekins in the freezer for at least 4 hours.

Pour a thin layer of melted chocolate onto a cookie sheet, and place in the refrigerator for at least 10 minutes until the chocolate has hardened. Grate the chocolate with a knife and set the shavings aside in the refrigerator.

When ready to serve, remove the wax paper strips from the ramekins. Garnish each soufflé with chocolate shavings, and sprinkle with cocoa.

CHEESE AND CHOCOLATE MOUSSE

6 SERVINGS

Preparation Time: 15 minutes
Cooking Time: 40 minutes

MOUSSE

3		medium eggs
1/2 cup	(125 ml)	sugar
1 1/2 cups	(375 ml)	hot milk
1/2 lb	(250 g)	cream cheese
4 oz	(125 g)	semisweet chocolate, melted
2 tbsp	(25 ml)	softened butter
3		slices of bread, cut into pieces
1 tbsp	(15 ml)	cocoa powder
1 tsp	(5 ml)	vanilla extract

GARNISH

2 oz	(60 g)	semi-sweet chocolate, melted
1/2 cup	(125 ml)	strawberry coulis
		fresh fruit, of choice
		chocolate shavings

MOUSSE

Preheat the oven to 350°F (180°C). In a food processor, or with an electric mixer, beat together the eggs and sugar. Incorporate the hot milk, cream cheese, melted chocolate, butter, bread, cocoa powder, and vanilla extract; mix well.

Pour the mixture into lightly buttered ramekins. Place the ramekins in a large ovenproof pan, and fill the pan with enough water so that the ramekins are partially submerged. Bake for 35 to 40 minutes. Let cool and remove from the ramekins.

GARNISH

Line the serving plates with melted chocolate and place the mousse in the center of the plates. Garnish with strawberry coulis, fresh fruit, and chocolate shavings.

MAPLE AND WHITE CHOCOLATE DELICACY

8 SERVINGS
Preparation Time: 25 minutes
Cooking Time: 30 minutes

MAPLE CAKE

2	medium eggs
3/4 cup	(175 ml) pure maple sugar
1/2 cup	(125 ml) softened butter
1/4 cup	(50 ml) milk
1/3 cup	(75 ml) all-purpose flour
2 tsp	(10 ml) baking powder
1	pinch of salt
1/2 cup	(125 ml) coarsely chopped walnuts
1/4 cup	(50 ml) boiling maple syrup

WHITE CHOCOLATE MOUSSE

8 oz	(250 g) white chocolate, melted
1/2 cup	(125 ml) 35% cream, whipped

GARNISH

4 oz	(125 g) white chocolate, melted

Preheat the oven to 350°F (180°C). With an electric mixer, beat together the eggs and the maple sugar until the mixture whitens. Incorporate the butter and mix. Add the milk, flour, baking powder and salt; mix for 1 to 2 minutes until the mixture is smooth. Add the walnuts and mix with a spatula. Pour into 8 small, greased and floured cake molds. Bake for 15 to 20 minutes. Let cool and remove from the molds. Drizzle with boiling maple syrup and set aside.

In a bowl, whip together the melted and lightly cooled chocolate with the whipped cream. Let cool until it reaches the consistency of mousse. Pour the mixture into a pastry bag with a star tip and garnish each small cake; set aside.

Pour the melted chocolate onto a cookie sheet and place in the refrigerator for 10 minutes. Create chocolate shavings by scraping the chocolate with a knife. Garnish the mousse with the white chocolate shavings and serve.

BLUEBERRY HONEY MOUSSE

4 SERVINGS
Preparation Time: 20 minutes
Cooking Time: none

2	medium egg yolks
1/4 cup	(50 ml) liquid blueberry honey
2	medium egg whites
1 cup	(250 ml) 35% cream
1/4 cup	(50 ml) blueberries, fresh or frozen

GARNISH

mint leaves

In a bowl, whip the egg yolks with the blueberry honey until the mixture whitens; set aside.

Whip the egg whites to form soft peaks.

With a spatula, mix together the egg whites and the yolk mixture.

Fold the whipped cream into the egg mixture.

Serve in champagne flutes and garnish with blueberries and fresh mint.

MOUSSES AND SOUFFLÉS

COFFEE ÉCLAIRS

8 SERVINGS

Preparation Time: 30 minutes
Cooking Time: 20 minutes

1 cup	(250 ml) water
1/3 cup	(75 ml) butter
1	pinch of salt
1 tbsp	(15 ml) sugar
2/3 cup	(150 ml) all-purpose flour
4	eggs

CREAM FILLING

2 cups	(500 ml) milk
1	square of unsweetened chocolate
1 tbsp	(15 ml) instant coffee granules
2	eggs
2	egg yolks
1/3 cup	(75 ml) sugar
1/3 cup	(75 ml) all-purpose flour
2 tbsp	(25 ml) butter
2 tbsp	(25 ml) coffee liqueur (Kahlua)

ICING

1/4 cup	(50 ml) very strong, hot, black coffee
2 tbsp	(25 ml) softened butter
1/2 cup	(125 ml) icing sugar

In a pan, bring the water, butter, salt and sugar to a boil. Remove the pan from the stove and add the flour all at once. Continue mixing until the dough is no longer sticking to the sides of the pan. Continue stirring while adding the eggs, one at a time. Place the dough in a pastry bag with a 1/2 in (1 cm) tip. Squeeze out 4 in (10 cm) long strips of dough onto a lightly greased cookie sheet. Bake for 15 to 20 minutes, or until puffy and golden. Remove from the oven and let cool.

In a saucepan, melt the chocolate and coffee in the milk. In a bowl, beat the whole eggs and the egg yolks with the sugar and flour. Add the warm milk mixture, and mix well. Add to the saucepan and cook over low heat. Stir continuously until the mixture thickens and sticks to the back of the spoon. Remove from the stove and add the butter and coffee liqueur; let cool. In a bowl, let the butter melt in the hot coffee and gradually add the icing sugar, while stirring. Mix well.

Make an incision on the side of each éclair, fill with cream filling and spread the icing on top. Refrigerate and serve.

CHOCOLATE PROFITEROLES

4 SERVINGS

Preparation Time: 20 minutes
Cooking Time: 20 minutes

12	small cream puffs
1 tbsp	(15 ml) cocoa powder
	fresh seasonal fruit, of choice

CRÈME ANGLAISE

4	medium egg yolks
1/2 cup	(125 ml) sugar
1 1/2 cups	(375 ml) warm milk
1/2 tsp	(2 ml) vanilla extract

CHOCOLATE CREAM

6 oz	(180 g) semi-sweet chocolate
2 tbsp	(25 ml) creamy peanut butter
1	small package of unflavored gelatin
2 tbsp	(25 ml) cold water
1/4 cup	(50 ml) hot water
2	eggs
1 cup	(250 ml) 35 % cream, whipped

GARNISH

	fresh fruit, of choice
	cocoa powder

CRÈME ANGLAISE

In a double boiler, mix together the eggs and sugar. Incorporate the warm milk and vanilla extract. Heat, while stirring continuously until the cream sticks to the back of the spoon. Pour into a bowl and refrigerate.

CHOCOLATE CREAM

In a saucepan, melt the chocolate and peanut butter; let cool. In a small bowl, let the gelatin stand in cold water. Then add hot water, mix and let cool.

In another bowl, whip the eggs, and incorporate the gelatin, chocolate and whipped cream. Mix well until smooth and refrigerate.

When the chocolate cream has set, cut the cream puffs in half and fill the center with the cream. Sprinkle with cocoa.

Line the serving plates with the crème anglaise and place 3 cream puffs on each plate. Garnish with fresh fruit.

SPRING BALLS

4 SERVINGS

Preparation Time: 15 minutes
Cooking Time: 7 minutes

1 cup	(250 ml) milk
1	pinch of salt
2 tbsp	(25 ml) sugar
1/4 cup	(50 ml) butter
1/2 tsp	(2 ml) vanilla extract
1/2 cup	(125 ml) all-purpose flour
3	medium eggs
1 tsp	(5 ml) orange zest
1 tsp	(5 ml) orange flavored flower water
	corn oil (for cooking)
	icing sugar, to taste

In a saucepan, combine the milk, salt, butter, and vanilla extract. Bring to a boil, remove from the stove and add the flour while stirring continuously with a wooden spoon.

Return to the stove and continue to stir until the dough becomes dry and is no longer sticking to the sides. Remove from the stove and incorporate the eggs, one at a time, taking care to mix well after each addition. Add the orange zest and the orange water and let set for a few minutes.

Heat a sufficient amount of oil in a deep fryer. Gently drop teaspoons of the dough into the hot oil. When the dough is puffy and golden, remove the balls from the deep fryer with a draining spoon. Pat dry with paper towel.

Serve the spring balls hot and sprinkle with icing sugar. Garnish with syrup.

CHOCOLATE AND PECAN CAPRICE

4 SERVINGS

Preparation Time: 15 minutes
Cooking Time: 15 minutes

2 tbsp	(25 ml) melted butter
6	sheets of philo pastry
1/4 cup	(50 ml) maple syrup
1 tbsp	(15 ml) cocoa powder
	fresh fruit, to garnish

CHOCOLATE FILLING

1/2 lb	(250 g) semi-sweet chocolate
2 tbsp	(25 ml) butter
2	medium eggs
1/2 cup	(125 ml) 35% cream, whipped
3/4 cup	(175 ml) chopped pecans

Preheat the oven to 350°F (180°C). On a flat surface, lightly brush 3 sheets of philo pastry with butter and place one on top of the other. Cut 6 circles of 4 to 5 in (10/11 cm) in diameter and place them on a greased cookie sheet. Brush with maple syrup and bake for 5 minutes. Repeat the process with the remaining philo pastry sheets and set aside.

CHOCOLATE FILLING

In a double boiler, or in a saucepan over very low heat, melt the chocolate and butter. Remove from the stove and incorporate the eggs. Let cool. Add the cream and pecans; mix and let cool for at least 30 minutes.

When ready to serve, spread half of the chocolate filling over 4 philo circles. Cover with another 4 philo circles and garnish with the remaining chocolate filling. Finish by covering with the remaining circles of philo and sprinkle with cocoa powder. Serve with fresh fruit.

CHOCOLATE CREAM CONES WITH MANGO COULIS

4 SERVINGS

Preparation Time: 1 hour
Cooking Time: 30 minutes

ALMOND CONES
1/4 cup (50 ml) all-purpose flour
1/4 cup (50 ml) icing sugar
1/4 cup (50 ml) butter
1 medium egg white
2 tbsp (25 ml) chopped almonds

CHOCOLATE CREAM
1/2 cup (125 ml) 35% cream
6 squares of semi-sweet chocolate, grated
1 tbsp (15 ml) butter

PUFF PASTRY
1/2 cup (125 ml) honey
1/4 cup (50 ml) water
3 sheets of philo pastry
2 tsp (10 ml) melted butter
1/2 cup (125 ml) pistachio nuts, peeled and chopped

MANGO COULIS
1/3 cup (75 ml) unsweetened orange juice
1 large mango, peeled and pitted
1 tbsp (15 ml) honey

GARNISH
1/4 cup (50 ml) pistachio nuts, peeled
4 clusters of fresh mint leaves
fresh fruit, of choice

ALMOND CONES

Preheat the oven to 350°F (180°C). With a food processor, or an electric mixer, mix together all of the ingredients, except for the almonds. With a spatula, shape four 5 in (13 cm), thin rounds of dough and place on a cookie sheet.

Sprinkle with almonds and bake for 4 to 5 minutes, or until golden. Remove from the oven and using a spatula, quickly shape into a cone; set aside.

CHOCOLATE CREAM

In a saucepan, heat the cream to a boiling point and remove from the stove. Incorporate the chocolate and butter and whip until the chocolate has completely melted. Let cool and beat with an electric mixer for 2 to 3 minutes or until the mixture forms soft peaks. Fill the cones with the cream and set aside.

PUFF PASTRY

In a saucepan, heat the honey and water; mix well and keep warm. On a work surface, brush 3 sheets of philo pastry with butter and place one on top of the other. Cut 12 rounds of pastry to fit your ramekins. Place one round of pastry on the bottom of each ramekin, brush with honey, and garnish with half of the pistachios. Cover with a second round of pastry and garnish as above, using the remaining pistachios. Finish with the remaining rounds and brush generously with honey. Bake for 12 to 15 minutes. Let cool and set aside.

MANGO COULIS

In another saucepan, simmer the orange juice, mango, and honey over medium heat for 2 minutes. With a food processor, or electric mixer, reduce to a purée. Pour into a bowl and set aside.

Line the serving plates with mango coulis. Place a puff pastry, accompanied with a cone on each plate. Garnish with pistachios, fresh fruits and mint leaves.

FLEETING MAPLE DREAMS

8 SERVINGS

Preparation Time: 20 minutes

Cooking Time: 2 hours

ALMOND AND MAPLE CAKE

2	large eggs
3/4 cup	(175 ml) maple sugar
1/2 cup	(125 ml) butter
1/4 cup	(50 ml) maple syrup
1/4 cup	(50 ml) milk
1/2 cup	(125 ml) all-purpose flour
1/2 cup	(125 ml) almond powder
2 tsp	(10 ml) baking powder
1	pinch of salt
1/4 cup	(50 ml) chocolate cream

MAPLE ICING

1/2 cup	(125 ml) maple syrup
2	large egg whites
2	large egg yolks
3/4 cup	(175 ml) 35% cream, whipped

GARNISH

1 cup	(250 ml) maple caramel
	fresh berries, of choice

ALMOND AND MAPLE CAKE

Preheat the oven to 350°F (180°C). With an electric mixer, beat together the eggs and maple sugar until white. Add the butter, maple syrup, milk, flour, almond powder, baking powder and salt. Beat until the mixture is smooth. Pour into 8 greased ramekins and bake for 25 to 30 minutes. Let cool. Remove from the ramekins and brush with chocolate cream.

MAPLE ICING

In a small saucepan, bring 1/2 of the maple syrup to a boil and let simmer over low heat for 3 to 4 minutes. Whip the egg whites to form soft peaks, and fold into the boiling maple syrup.

With an electric mixer, whip together the egg yolks and the remaining maple syrup. Add the whipped cream and the egg white preparation. Mix with a spatula or wooden spoon. Freeze for 1 to 2 hours.

When ready to serve, line the plates with maple caramel and berries. Cut the small cakes in half and ice the center.

PARTIAL TO CHOCOLATE DESSERT

8 SERVINGS

Preparation Time: 15 minutes
Cooking Time: 30 minutes

1 cup	(250 ml) sugar
3/4 cup	(175 ml) butter
1 tsp	(5 ml) vanilla extract
2	medium eggs
1/4 cup	(50 ml) sour cream
1 1/2 cups	(375 ml) flour
2 tbsp	(25 ml) cocoa powder
1 tsp	(5 ml) baking soda
1/2 cup	(125 ml) semi-sweet chocolate, cut into pieces
2 cups	(500 ml) 35% cream, with 2 tbsp (25 ml) icing sugar
1/4 cup	(50 ml) cocoa powder

GARNISH

1/4 cup	(50 ml) pecans or walnuts
1/2 cup	(125 ml) chocolate shavings

Preheat the oven to 350°F (180°C). With a food processor or an electric mixer, mix together the sugar, butter, and vanilla extract for 1 to 2 minutes until the mixture whitens.

Incorporate the eggs, one at a time, and mix. Add the sour cream, flour, cocoa powder and baking soda. Mix for 1 to 2 minutes, or until the mixture is smooth.

Pour the mixture into 2 greased and floured 8 in (20 cm) cake molds. Bake for 25 to 30 minutes (prick with a toothpick; if the toothpick comes out clean, the cake is ready). Let cool and remove from the cake molds.

In a saucepan, melt the chocolate. Remove from the stove, and let cool. In a bowl, mix together the cream, cocoa powder and cooled, melted chocolate.

Garnish the top of one cake with the chocolate cream and place the second cake on top. Spread the remaining chocolate cream all over the cake. Sprinkle nuts and chocolate shavings on top.

DOUBLE CHOCOLATE CHARLOTTE

8 SERVINGS

Preparation Time: 25 minutes
Refrigeration Time: 2 to 3 hours

1/2 lb	(250 g) lady finger biscuits
4 oz	(125 g) white chocolate
4 oz	(125 g) semi-sweet chocolate
2	packages of unflavored gelatin
1/4 cup	(50 ml) cold water
1/2 cup	(125 ml) hot water
1 1/2 cups	(375 ml) 35% cream
1/4 cup	(50 ml) cocoa powder

CRÈME ANGLAISE

6	medium egg yolks
3/4 cup	(175 ml) sugar
2 cups	(500 ml) hot milk
1 tsp	(5 ml) vanilla extract

Trim one end of each biscuit. Line the inside rim of a charlotte pan, or any round mold with the biscuits.

CRÈME ANGLAISE

In a double boiler or in a saucepan, over very low heat, mix together the egg yolks and sugar. Add the warm milk and vanilla extract. Stir continuously until the cream sticks to the back of a wooden spoon. Remove from the stove, and pour into two bowls. Set aside.

In separate saucepans, melt the white chocolate and semi-sweet chocolate, over very low heat. In a bowl, let the gelatin stand in cold water and then mix with the hot water. Add the gelatin to the two bowls of egg mixture. Add melted chocolate to each of the bowls. When it begins to set, add whipped cream to each bowl, mix until it becomes smooth.

Pour the Crème Anglaise into the charlotte pan; first the white, then the brown. Let set for a few hours in the refrigerator. Sprinkle with cocoa powder.

IRRESISTIBLE MOKA CAKE

8 TO 10 SERVINGS

Preparation Time: 40 minutes
Cooking Time: 35 minutes

SPONGE CAKE

1/2 cup	(125 ml)	sugar
4		eggs
1 tsp	(5 ml)	vanilla extract
1		pinch of salt
3/4 cup	(175 ml)	all-purpose flour
1/4 cup	(50 ml)	cocoa powder
1/2 cup	(125 ml)	melted butter

COFFEE MOUSSE

1 tbsp	(15 ml)	gelatin
1/4 cup	(50 ml)	cold water
2 tbsp	(25 ml)	instant coffee granules
1 cup	(250 ml)	boiling water
2		egg yolks
2/3 cup	(150 ml)	brown sugar
1		pinch of salt
2		egg whites
1 cup	(250 ml)	35% cream

ORANGE SYRUP

1/2 cup	(125 ml)	water
1/2 cup	(125 ml)	sugar
		zest of 2 oranges, blanched
2 tbsp	(25 ml)	orange maple liqueur

CHOCOLATE CREAM

12 oz	(350 g)	melted chocolate
2/3 cup	(150 ml)	35% cream
2 tbsp	(25 ml)	butter

SPONGE CAKE

Place the sugar and the eggs in a double boiler. Heat and whisk together for 10 minutes until the mixture becomes very fluffy and doubles in volume. Add the vanilla and salt.

Remove from the stove and slowly sift in the flour and cocoa. Add the melted butter and let cool. Pour into 2 greased and floured cake pans and bake at 350°F (180°C) for approximately 25 minutes.

COFFEE MOUSSE

Let the gelatin set in cold water. Dilute the coffee granules in boiling water. Beat the egg yolks, brown sugar and salt together.

Add the coffee to the egg yolk mixture and cook until it thickens. Add the gelatin and mix well, making sure that the gelatin completely dissolves.

Beat the egg whites and fold into the coffee mixture. Then add the cream to the mixture.

ORANGE SYRUP

Boil the water, sugar and orange zest for 10 minutes. Let cool and strain. Add the orange liqueur and soak the cakes with the syrup. Store the remaining liquid in the refrigerator.

CHOCOLATE CREAM

Heat the cream and add the chocolate; mix well and add the butter. Mix until the butter has melted completely. Let cool at room temperature until the mixture is lightly set and easy to spread.

In a double boiler, melt 4 oz (125 g) of white chocolate and pour onto a cookie sheet. Let cool. Using a serrated knife, scrape the chocolate to create chocolate shavings, and set aside.

Cut the cakes in two, garnish the center with coffee mousse. Ice the cake with the chocolate cream and sprinkle with chocolate shavings.

UPSIDE DOWN STRAWBERRY CHEESE CAKE

12 SERVINGS

Preparation Time: 15 minutes
Cooking Time: 1 hour

STRAWBERRY PREPARATION
12 oz	(375 ml)	cream cheese
1/3 cup	(75 ml)	all-purpose flour
10 oz	(300 g)	strawberries, fresh or frozen
2 tbsp	(25 ml)	honey (optional)

CAKE
2		medium eggs
1 1/2 cups	(375 ml)	sugar
1/2 cup	(125 ml)	soft butter
2/3 cup	(150 ml)	all-purpose flour
4 tsp	(20 ml)	baking powder
2/3 cup	(150 ml)	almond powder
2 tsp	(10 ml)	vanilla extract

GARNISH
10		strawberries, sliced
1/3 cup	(75 ml)	blueberries

STRAWBERRY COULIS
10 oz	(300 g)	strawberries, fresh or frozen
1 tbsp	(15 ml)	honey
1/2 cup	(125 ml)	unsweetened apple juice

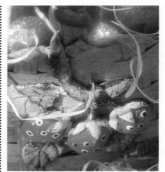

STRAWBERRY PREPARATION

Preheat the oven to 350°F (180°C). In a large bowl, mix together the eggs, cheese and flour. Add the strawberries and honey; mix delicately with a spatula. Pour into a round, greased 9 in (23 cm) cake mold; set aside.

CAKE

With a food processor or an electric mixer, mix together all the ingredients of the cake: the egg, sugar, flour, baking powder, almond powder, butter, and vanilla extract. Beat for 2 to 3 minutes until the mixture is smooth.

Pour the cake mixture over the strawberry preparation and bake for approximately 45 to 55 minutes. Let cool for 30 minutes and remove from the mold. Garnish with strawberries and blueberries.

STRAWBERRY COULIS

In a saucepan, simmer the strawberries, honey and apple juice over low heat for 2 minutes. Using a food processor or an electric mixer, purée the mixture and strain.

Serve the cake garnished with the strawberry coulis.

CHESTNUT CHARLOTTE

10 SERVINGS

Preparation Time: 30 minutes
Refrigeration Time: 2 to 3 hours

MAPLE CRÈME ANGLAISE

6	egg yolks
1/2 cup	(125 ml) maple syrup
1 1/2 cups	(375 ml) milk
1 tsp	(5 ml) vanilla extract
1 tsp	(5 ml) cornstarch, diluted in a little water

BAVARIAN CHESTNUT CREAM

1 1/2 cups	(375 ml) 35% cream
1/3 cup	(75 ml) icing sugar
2	packages of unflavored gelatin
1/4 cup	(50 ml) cold water
1/2 cup	(125 ml) boiling water
14 oz	(398 ml) chestnut purée

GARNISH

1	box of lady finger biscuits (rolled in chocolate)

MAPLE CRÈME ANGLAISE

In a double boiler or saucepan, mix together the egg yolks and maple syrup. Add the warm milk, vanilla and cornstarch. Heat and stir continuously until the cream sticks to the back of the spoon. Pour into a large bowl, and let cool.

BAVARIAN CHESTNUT CREAM

In a bowl, whisk together the cream and sugar; set aside.

In a small bowl, let the gelatin set in cold water and then add the boiling water; mix well. Pour the maple crème anglaise into the chestnut cream mixture and mix well.

When the chestnut cream begins to set, use a spatula to fold it into the whipped cream.

Line the inside rim of a charlotte pan or a round pan with the lady finger biscuits. Pour the Bavarian chestnut cream into the pan and refrigerate for approximately 2 to 3 hours. Remove from the pan and garnish with chocolate shavings.

MAJESTIC CAKE

12 SERVINGS

Preparation Time: 30 minutes
Cooking Time: 45 to 55 minutes

1/3 cup	(75 ml) maple syrup
2	apples, diced
3/4 cup	(175 ml) chopped pecans
3	eggs
3/4 cup	(175 ml) sugar
1/2 cup	(125 ml) butter
1/4 cup	(50 ml) milk
3/4 cup	(175 ml) all-purpose flour
1 tbsp	(15 ml) baking powder
1	pinch of salt

MAPLE ICING

1/2 cup	(125 ml) unsalted butter
4 cups	(1 L) icing sugar
1/2 cup	(125 ml) maple syrup

GARNISH

chocolate sauce
berries, of choice

In a saucepan, reduce the maple syrup by one half and add the pecans. Let simmer for 1 to 2 minutes and set aside.

Preheat the oven to 350°F (180°C). With an electric mixer, beat together the eggs and sugar until white. Incorporate the butter and mix. Then add the milk and dry ingredients, alternating between the two.

Add the apples to the maple syrup and pecan mixture. Pour the mixture into a greased and floured, crown shaped mold (ie. an angel food cake mold). Bake for 45 to 55 minutes. Let cool and remove from the mold.

When serving, pour hot chocolate sauce over the cake and garnish the center with berries.

COFFEE LIQUEUR CAKE

10 TO 12 SERVINGS

Preparation Time: 45 minutes
Cooking Time: 30 to 40 minutes

3/4 cup	(175 ml) cocoa powder
1 tsp	(5 ml) instant coffee
1 cup	(250 ml) boiling water
1/2 cup	(125 ml) coffee liqueur (Kahlua)
1/2 cup	(125 ml) softened butter
1/4 cup	(50 ml) shortening
1 3/4 cups	(425 ml) sugar
3	eggs
1 tsp	(5 ml) vanilla extract
2 cups	(500 ml) all-purpose flour
2 tsp	(10 ml) baking powder
1 tsp	(5 ml) salt
1/2 tsp	(2 ml) baking soda

ICING

6	squares of semi-sweet chocolate
1 cup	(250 ml) butter
1/4 cup	(50 ml) coffee liqueur (Kahlua)
1/4 cup	(50 ml) 35% cream
1 1/2 cups	(375 ml) icing sugar

Preheat the oven to 350°F (180°C). Grease and flour an angel food cake mold. In a small bowl, mix together, the cocoa, coffee and boiling water; mix well. Add the coffee liqueur and let cool.

In a large bowl, beat together the butter, shortening, sugar, eggs and vanilla. In another bowl, mix together the flour, baking powder, salt and baking soda.

Add the butter and liquid mixtures to the flour mixture. Mix well between each addition. Pour into the cake pan and bake for 30 to 40 minutes or until an inserted toothpick comes out clean. Let cool and remove from the pan.

Meanwhile, prepare the icing. In a saucepan, mix together the chocolate, butter, coffee liqueur and cream. Cook over low heat until the chocolate has melted completely. Remove from the stove and add the icing sugar. Let cool, while beating a few times.

Cut the cake in large layers and spread the icing between each layer, as well as on top.

HONEY LOAF

8 TO 10 PORTIONS

Preparation Time: 15 minutes
Cooking Time: 2 hours

1 3/4 cups	(425 ml) all-purpose flour
1/2 tsp	(2 ml) ground cinnamon
1	pinch of ground clove
1	pinch of ground nutmeg
1 tsp	(5 ml) baking powder
1	pinch of salt
1/4 cup	(50 ml) butter
2 tbsp	(25 ml) mayonnaise
1/4 cup	(50 ml) brown sugar
2/3 cup	(150 ml) milk
1/2 cup	(125 ml) honey

GARNISH

1/4 cup	(50 ml) sliced almonds

Preheat the oven to 325°F (160°C). Grease and flour a 8 1/2 x 4 1/2 in (21 x 6.5 cm) loaf pan.

In a bowl, mix together the flour, cinnamon, ground clove, nutmeg, baking powder, and salt. Add the butter, mayonnaise, and brown sugar. Mix so that the mixture remains lumpy. Add the milk and honey; mix well.

Pour the mixture into the loaf pan and sprinkle the top with sliced almonds. Bake for 1 hour 45 minutes to 2 hours, or until a knife, inserted in the center, comes out clean.

Let cool for 5 minutes. Remove from the pan and serve warm or cold.

DOUBLE CHOCOLATE MARBLE CAKE

12 SERVINGS
Preparation Time: 45 minutes
Cooking Time: 40 to 45 minutes

MARBLE CAKE

3	eggs
1 cup	(250 ml) sugar
1 cup	(250 ml) butter
	a few drops of vanilla extract
2 cups	(500 ml) flour
1 tbsp	(15 ml) baking powder
1/2 tsp	(2 ml) salt
1 cup	(250 ml) milk
6 oz	(175 g) semi-sweet chocolate, melted

CHOCOLATE ICING

1 cup	(250 ml) 35% cream
3/4 cup	(175 ml) icing sugar
2 tbsp	(25 ml) cocoa powder
2 oz	(60 g) semi-sweet chocolate, melted

CHOCOLATE GARNISH

8 oz	(250 g) dark chocolate, melted
8 oz	(250 g) white chocolate, melted

MARBLE CAKE

Preheat the oven to 350°F (180°C). In a bowl, use an electric mixer to beat together the eggs and sugar until white. Then add the butter and vanilla, mix well. In another bowl, mix together the flour, baking powder and salt. Sift and add to the first mixture, alternating with the milk. Pour into a greased and floured, 9 in (23 cm) cake pan. Pour the melted chocolate into the cake mixture and mix with a fork or knife in order to obtain a marble look. Bake for approximately 40 to 45 minutes. Let cool and remove from the pan.

In a bowl, whip the cream with an electric mixer. Add the icing sugar, cocoa, and melted chocolate; set aside.

CHOCOLATE GARNISH

Pour the melted dark chocolate onto the bottom of a cookie sheet and let cool. Once it has hardened, cut into triangles. Repeat the same process with the white chocolate. Ice the cake and garnish with chocolate triangles.

RASPBERRY LAYERED CAKE

8 TO 12 SERVINGS
Preparation Time: 25 minutes
Cooking Time: 15 minutes

1/2 cup	(125 ml) icing sugar
3	medium egg yolks
1/3 cup	(75 ml) potato starch
3	medium egg whites
1 1/2 cups	(375 ml) raspberry jam
1 1/2 cups	(375 ml) semi-sweet chocolate chips
2 tbsp	(25 ml) icing sugar

SOFT ICING

1/4 cup	(50 ml) water
1/4 cup	(50 ml) corn syrup
1/4 cup	(50 ml) chopped, unsweetened chocolate
2 3/4 cups	(675 ml) sifted icing sugar

Preheat the oven to 400°F (200°C). In a bowl, mix together the icing sugar and the egg yolks until the mixture thickens. Add the potato starch and mix well.

With a whisk, or an electric mixer, whip the egg whites to form soft peaks. Slowly add the egg whites to the egg yolk mixture. Pour into three 8 in (20 cm) round cake pans. Bake for 13 to 15 minutes.

SOFT ICING

In a saucepan, combine the water, corn syrup, and chocolate and bring to a boil. Remove from the stove and add the icing sugar, in two steps. Blend well between each addition. The mixture should be smooth and liquid.

Remove the cakes from the molds. Place one of the cakes on top of a cooling rack, placed on top of a cookie sheet, and garnish with half of the raspberry jam. Place a second cake on top and garnish with the remaining raspberry jam. Finish by placing the third and final cake on top.

Pour the soft icing over the cake. Make sure that the entire cake is covered. Garnish with chocolate chips and sprinkle with icing sugar.

CHEESECAKE WITH RHUBARB AND STRAWBERRY SAUCE

4 SERVINGS

Preparation Time: 15 minutes
Cooking Time: 15 minutes

CRUST
1 cup	(250 ml) bread crumbs
2 tbsp	(25 ml) grated almonds or hazelnuts
1/4 cup	(50 ml) butter
1 tbsp	(15 ml) brown sugar

FILLING
2	packages of unflavored gelatin
1 cup	(250 ml) apple juice
3 cups	(750 ml) cottage cheese
2	bananas
1/4 cup	(50 ml) sugar

SAUCE
2 cups	(500 ml) rhubarb
1 cup	(250 ml) sliced strawberries
3/4 cup	(175 ml) sugar
2 tbsp	(25 ml) orange liqueur (optional)
2 tbsp	(25 ml) cornstarch

GARNISH
1/2 cup	(125 ml) grated coconut
	zest of lemon or lime
	sliced strawberries

CRUST

With a food processor, mix together all the ingredients of the crust. Use your fingers to press out the crust, covering the bottom of a 9 in (23 cm) pie plate.

FILLING

In a measuring cup, sprinkle the gelatin into 1/4 cup (50 ml) of apple juice. Let stand for 5 minutes. Place the measuring cup in a pan of hot water, and heat slowly until the gelatin has dissolved completely. Remove from the hot water and set aside.

In a food processor, mix together the cottage cheese, bananas, sugar, and the remaining apple juice until you obtain a smooth mixture. Add the gelatin and mix. Pour over the crust, and let set in the refrigerator for 3 to 4 hours, or until the mixture is firm.

SAUCE

In a saucepan, combine the rhubarb, strawberries, sugar, and orange liqueur (optional). Bring to a boil over medium-high heat. Reduce the heat and simmer for approximately 5 minutes. Thicken with cornstarch that has been diluted in a little cold water; mix well.

Remove the cake from the pie plate, cover with sauce, and sprinkle with coconut. Garnish with lemon zest and slices of strawberries.

SPECIAL OCCASION BROWNIES

10 SERVINGS

Preparation Time: 20 minutes
Cooking Time: 45 minutes

BROWNIES

2	medium eggs
3/4 cup	(175 ml) softened butter
1/4 cup	(50 ml) milk
1/2 cup	(125 ml) all-purpose flour
1 tsp	(5 ml) baking powder
1/3 cup	(75 ml) almond powder
1/4 cup	(50 ml) cocoa powder
4 oz	(125 g) semi-sweet chocolate, melted
1 cup	(250 ml) pecans

CHOCOLATE MOUSSE

4	medium egg yolks
1/2 cup	(125 ml) sugar
1 1/2 cups	(375 ml) warm milk
1 tsp	(5 ml) cornstarch, diluted in a little water
1 tsp	(5 ml) vanilla extract
2	packages of unflavored gelatin
1/4 cup	(50 ml) cold water
1/2 cup	(125 ml) boiling water
12 oz	(375 g) melted chocolate
1 cup	(250 ml) 35% cream, whipped

GARNISH

chocolate chips

BROWNIES

Preheat the oven to 350°F (180°C). With an electric mixer, mix together the eggs and sugar. Incorporate the butter, flour, milk, baking powder and chocolate. Then add the pecans and mix well. Pour the mixture into a greased and floured 9 in (23 cm) cake pan. Bake for 30 to 35 minutes. Set aside and let cool.

CHOCOLATE MOUSSE

In a double boiler or in a saucepan, over low heat, combine the egg yolks and the sugar. Add the warm milk, cornstarch and vanilla extract. Stir continuously and heat until the mixture sticks to the back of the spoon. Pour into a large bowl and let cool.

In a small bowl, let the gelatin set in the cold water for a few minutes and then add the boiling water. Add the gelatin and melted chocolate to the chocolate mousse.

Refrigerate for 10 to 15 minutes. When the mixture starts to set, incorporate the whipped cream. Pour the mixture into the cake pan and let set in the refrigerator for 1 to 2 hours.

When serving, garnish with chocolate chips.

CHOCOLATE CRANBERRY CAKE

8 TO 10 SERVINGS

Preparation Time: 20 minutes
Cooking Time: 50 minutes

CAKE

2	medium eggs	
1 cup	(250 ml) sugar	
3/4 cup	(175 ml) butter	
1 tsp	(5 ml) vanilla extract	
1/4 cup	(50 ml) sour cream	
1 1/2 cups	(375 ml) all-purpose flour	
1/4 cup	(50 ml) cocoa	
1/2 cup	(125 ml) chopped walnuts	
1 tsp	(5 ml) baking soda	

CRANBERRIES

1 1/2 cups	(375 ml) cranberries	
3/4 cup	(175 ml) unsweetened orange juice	
1/4 cup	(50 ml) sugar	
1 tbsp	(15 ml) unflavored gelatin	
2 tbsp	(25 ml) cold water	
2 tbsp	(25 ml) warm water	

ICING

1 lb	(500 g) semi-sweet chocolate	
1 cup	(250 ml) 35% cream, hot	
1/4 cup	(50 ml) corn syrup	

GARNISH

fresh fruit

CAKE

Preheat the oven to 350°F (180°C). In a food processor, mix together the egg, sugar, butter and vanilla extract for 1 to 2 minutes, or until the mixture has whitened.

Incorporate the sour cream, flour, cocoa, walnuts and baking soda. Mix for 1 to 2 minutes, or until the mixture becomes uniform.

Pour the mixture into 2 round greased and floured 8 in (20 cm) cake pans. Bake for 30 to 35 minutes. Let cool and remove from the pans.

CRANBERRIES

In a saucepan, simmer the cranberries over low heat for 5 minutes and set aside. Combine the cranberries, orange juice and sugar. Let the gelatin set in cold water for a few minutes, then add the warm water. Add the gelatin to the cranberry mixture and let cool. Set aside.

ICING

In a double boiler, or in a saucepan, melt the chocolate over very low heat. Add the hot cream and corn syrup. Whip until the mixture becomes smooth and uniform.

Pour into a bowl and let cool. Cover the bowl with plastic wrap and set aside at room temperature.

Place the first layer of cake on a plate, fill with cranberries and cover with the second layer of cake. Let set in the refrigerator for 20 minutes. Spread the chocolate icing over the cooled cake and garnish with fresh fruits.

CREAMY CHOCOLATE CAKE

10 SERVING

Preparation Time: 25 minutes
Cooking Time: 20 minutes

2 cups	(500 ml) graham cracker crumbs
1/2 cup	(125 ml) melted butter
1/4 cup	(50 ml) maple syrup
2	packages of unflavored gelatin
1/4 cup	(50 ml) cold water
1/3 cup	(75 ml semi-sweet chocolate, melted
1 1/2 cups	(375 ml) 35% cream, whipped

CRÈME ANGLAISE

4	egg yolks
1/2 cup	(125) sugar
1 cup	(250 ml) warm milk
1 tsp	(5 ml) vanilla extract
1/2 tsp	(2 ml) cornstarch diluted in a little milk

GARNISH

chocolate shavings

Preheat the oven to 350°F (180°C). In a bowl, mix together the graham cracker crumbs, melted butter and maple syrup. Place in the bottom of a lightly buttered, round 9 in (23 cm) cake pan. Bake in the oven for 10 minutes and let cool.

CRÈME ANGLAISE

In a double boiler or in a saucepan, mix together the egg whites and the sugar and cook over low heat until the mixture whitens. Add the warm milk, vanilla extract and cornstarch. Cook until the cream sticks to the back of the spoon. Pour into a large bowl and let cool.

In a small bowl, let the gelatin set in cold water for a few minutes and mix with the boiling water. Pour into the Crème Anglaise and add the melted chocolate; mix well.

Once the cream starts to set (place in the refrigerator if necessary) incorporate the whipped cream and mix with a spatula. Pour into the cake pan and place in the refrigerator for 2 to 3 hours.

Remove from the pan and garnish with chocolate shavings.

PEACH SPONGE CAKE WITH BEER

4 SERVINGS

Preparation Time: 10 minutes
Cooking Time: 45 minutes

12 oz	(341 ml) beer
1/2 cup	(125 ml) sugar
6	medium eggs
1 cup	(250 ml) all-purpose flour
1	pinch of salt
3/4 cup	(175 ml) milk
19 oz	(540 ml) can of peaches, cut in half and drained

In a pan, combine the beer and sugar, and bring to a boil. Let reduce by 75%, and refrigerate. Preheat the oven to 375°F (190°C). In a bowl, combine the eggs, beer, flour, salt and milk; mix well.

Pour into a greased 9 in (23 cm) quiche dish. Garnish with peaches, and bake for approximately 40 to 45 minutes.

GRAND MARNIER STRAWBERRY COCKTAIL

4 TO 6 SERVINGS

Preparation Time: 15 minutes
Refrigeration Time: 1 to 2 hours

2 cups	(500 ml) fresh strawberries
1/4 cup	(50 ml) sugar
	zest of 1 orange
1/2 cup	(125 ml) Grand Marnier
1 1/2 cups	(375 ml) 35% cream
GARNISH	
	roasted pistachios or almonds

In a large bowl, mix together the strawberries, sugar, orange zest and Grand Marnier. Refrigerate for 1 to 2 hours.

In another bowl, whip the cream until it becomes firm.

Incorporate the strawberries to the whipped cream. Pour into large dessert cups and garnish with pistachios or almonds.

PEARS GLAZED WITH BEER

4 SERVINGS

Preparation Time: 10 minutes

Cooking Time: 20 minutes

12 oz (341 ml) beer
1 cup (250 ml) maple syrup
1 cup (250 ml) apple jelly
4 pears, peeled

CRÈME ANGLAISE
6 medium egg yolks
3/4 cup (175 ml) sugar
2 cups (500 ml) hot milk
1 tsp (5 ml) vanilla extract

In a saucepan, bring the beer to a boil and reduce by half. Add the maple syrup, apple jelly and pears. Cover and let simmer over low heat for 10 to 12 minutes, turning the pears if necessary.

Remove the pears from the saucepan and set aside. Return the saucepan to the stove and simmer the sauce until it thickens. Pour over the pears.

CRÈME ANGLAISE

In a double boiler or in a saucepan over low heat, mix together the egg yolks and sugar. Add the hot milk and the vanilla extract. Stir constantly and cook until the cream sticks to the back of a wooden spoon. Remove from the stove and set aside.

Serve the pears with the syrup or crème anglaise.

VANILLA PEACHES

4 SERVINGS

Preparation Time: 15 minutes

Cooking Time: 15 minutes

CRÈME ANGLAISE
4 egg yolks
1/3 cup (75 ml) sugar
1 cup (250 ml) hot milk
1/2 tsp (2 ml) cornstarch, diluted
in a little milk
1 tsp (5 ml) vanilla extract

RASPBERRY COULIS
1 cup (250 ml) raspberries
1/4 cup (50 ml) apple juice
1 tsp (5 ml) lemon juice (optional)
1/4 cup (50 ml) sugar

GARNISH
2 English muffins, cut in half and
lightly toasted
4 half peaches
4 sprigs of fresh mint

CRÈME ANGLAISE

In a double boiler or in a saucepan, over low heat, mix together the egg yolks and the sugar. Add the hot milk, cornstarch and vanilla extract. Cook until the cream sticks to back of a wooden spoon, stirring constantly. Pour into a large bowl and refrigerate.

RASPBERRY COULIS

In a small saucepan, combine the raspberries, apple juice, lemon juice and sugar. Bring to a boil and let simmer for 2 to 3 minutes over low heat. Reduce to a purée in a food processor and strain; set aside.

GARNISH

Place the halved muffins in the middle of the plates. Cover the muffins and the plate with the raspberry coulis. Garnish the muffins with peaches and cover with crème anglaise and mint leaves.

VANILLA SUMMER DELIGHT

4 TO 6 SERVINGS

Preparation Time: 15 minutes
Cooking Time: none

1 1/2 cups	(375 ml) 35% cream
1 1/2 cups	(375 ml) mixed berries
1/2 cup	(125 ml) Oreo cookies, crushed

GARNISH

berries
mint leaves
cookies of choice

In a bowl, whip the cream until it becomes firm.

Incorporate the berries and cookies; mix gently. Pour into large dessert cups. Garnish with berries, mint leaves and whole cookies.

A NEST OF ICE CREAM AND PEARS

4 SERVINGS

Preparation Time: 10 minutes
Cooking Time: 10 minutes

6 oz	(180 g.) semi-sweet chocolate, cut into small pieces
1/2 cup	(125 ml) 15% cream
2	English muffins, cut in half and lightly toasted
4	scoops of vanilla ice cream
4	half pears
1/4 cup	(50 ml) sliced almonds, lightly roasted

GARNISH

berries (strawberries, raspberries, blueberries, etc.)
mint leaves

In a small saucepan, over low heat, melt the chocolate and add the cream; mix well until smooth. Keep warm.

Place the halved muffins in the center of four plates. Garnish with a scoop of vanilla ice cream, half a pear, chocolate sauce and toasted almonds.

Garnish with berries and mint leaves.

FRUITY DESSERTS

APPLE AND BLACKBERRY LIQUEUR DESSERT

4 SERVINGS

Preparation Time: 15 minutes

Cooking Time: 50 minutes

4		slices of bread
1 tbsp	(15 ml)	butter
3		medium eggs
1 1/2 cups	(375 ml)	milk
1/4 cup	(50 ml)	corn syrup
2 tbsp	(25 ml)	chopped walnuts
2 tbsp	(25 ml)	blackberry liqueur
2		apples, peeled, cored and thinly sliced into rings

Preheat the oven to 375°F (190°C). Spread butter on both sides of the bread slices and place in 4 ovenproof ramekins. Bake for 2 minutes until lightly golden. Set aside.

In a bowl, mix together the eggs, milk, corn syrup, walnuts and blackberry liqueur; set aside.

Garnish each ramekin with rounds of apple and the blackberry liquor mix. Bake for 35 to 45 minutes.

STRAWBERRY COCKTAIL WITH SABAYON AND BLACKBERRY LIQUEUR

4 SERVINGS

Preparation Time: 10 minutes

Cooking Time: 15 minutes

5		egg yolks
1/2 cup	(125 ml)	sugar
1/2 cup	(125 ml)	dry white wine
1/2 cup	(125 ml)	blackberry liqueur
1 1/2 cups	(375 ml)	fresh strawberries, cut in half

GARNISH

4	clusters of mint leaves
4	thin biscuits

Whip together the egg yolks and sugar. Place in a double boiler and cook over low heat, while stirring continuously.

When the mixture has whitened, add the white wine and blackberry liqueur. Whip until it becomes a thick cream.

Remove from the stove and pour into dessert cups. Garnish with strawberries, mint leaves and thin biscuits.

HONEY FROSTED KIWIS

6 TO 8 SERVINGS

Preparation Time: 15 minutes

Freezing Time: 2 to 3 hours

3	medium egg yolks
1/4 cup	(50 ml) honey
1 1/2 cups	(375 ml) buttermilk, hot
1 tbsp	(15 ml) cornstarch, diluted in a bit of water
1/3 cup	(75 ml) apple juice
2	egg whites, whipped to form soft peaks
4 to 6	kiwis, peeled and diced
	zest of 1 orange
	zest of 1 lemon
1	grapefruit, cut into wedges
6 to 8	strawberries
6 to 8	sprigs of fresh mint (optional)

In a double boiler or in a saucepan over low heat, mix together the egg yolks and 1 tbsp (15 ml) of honey. Add the hot buttermilk and cornstarch. Mix well and cook until the cream sticks to the back of a wooden spoon. Let cool and set aside.

In a small saucepan, bring the apple juice and remaining honey to a boil.

Mix well and slowly pour the boiling syrup into the egg whites, while whipping; set aside.

In a large bowl, mix together the cream, egg whites, kiwis and zests.

Pour into ramekins, or small dessert cups, and freeze for 2 to 3 hours.

When serving, remove from the ramekins or dessert cups. Garnish with grapefruit, strawberries and mint leaves.

PEARS WITH CRÈME ANGLAISE

4 TO 6 SERVINGS
Preparation Time: 25 minutes
Cooking Time: 35 minutes

ALMOND CAKE
2	eggs
3/4 cup	(175 ml) sugar
1/2 cup	(125 ml) butter
1/4 cup	(50 ml) milk
1/3 cup	(75 ml) all purpose flour
1/2 tsp	(2 ml) baking powder
1/2 cup	(125 ml) almond powder

CRÈME ANGLAISE
4	egg yolks
1/2 cup	(125 ml) sugar
1 cup	(250 ml) hot milk
1/4 cup	(50 ml) blackberry liqueur
1 tsp	(5 ml) cornstarch, diluted in a little water
1 tsp	(5 ml) vanilla extract
1/4 cup	(125 ml) 35% cream, whipped
6	pear halves

GARNISH
	berries, of choice
6	sprigs of mint

ALMOND CAKE

Preheat the oven to 350°F (180°C). Beat together the eggs and sugar with an electric mixer. Add the butter, milk, flour, baking powder, and almond powder. Beat until all the ingredients are completely blended together. Pour the mixture into a greased and floured muffin pan (with 6 cups). Bake for 20 minutes. Let cool, remove from the pan and set aside.

CRÈME ANGLAISE

In a double boiler or saucepan over low heat, mix together the eggs and sugar. Add the hot milk, blackberry liqueur, cornstarch and vanilla. Cook until the mixture is thick and remove from the stove. Pour into a large bowl and let cool.

Gently mix together the crème anglaise and whipped cream and set aside. Place each small cake on a serving plate and garnish with a half pear. Cover with cream. Decorate with berries and a sprig of fresh mint.

STRAWBERRIES WITH WINE AND PEPPERCORNS

6 SERVINGS
Preparation Time: 10 minutes
Cooking Time: 5 minutes

1/4 cup	(50 ml) icing sugar
1 tsp	(5 ml) crushed pink peppercorns
1 tsp	(5 ml) crushed black peppercorns
2/3 cup	(150 ml) water
2/3 cup	(150 ml) white wine
1 lb	(454 g) strawberries, quartered

GARNISH
	mint leaves

In a saucepan, mix together the icing sugar, pink and black peppercorns, and water and bring to a boil. Set aside and let cool.

Add the wine and strawberries to the mixture. Mix well and refrigerate for 1 hour.

Serve in dessert cups and garnish with fresh mint leaves.

VANILLA PEARS

6 SERVINGS

Preparation Time: 20 minutes

Cooking Time: 15 minutes

6	pears
1/4 cup	(50 ml) butter
1/2 cup	(125 ml) sugar
1	pie dough

CRÈME ANGLAISE

4	medium egg yolks
1/2 cup	(125 ml) sugar
1 1/2 cups	(375 ml) hot milk
1 tsp	(5 ml) vanilla extract

Preheat the oven to 350°F (180°C). Peel the pears, remove the pits and cut into quarters.

In an ovenproof pan, melt the butter and sugar. Slowly increase the intensity of the heat and lightly caramelize the sugar. Add the pears and cook for 5 minutes.

Cover the pears with the pie dough and bake in the oven for 15 minutes or until the dough is golden. Let set for 5 minutes and remove from the pie plate by turning upside down onto a serving plate.

CRÈME ANGLAISE

In a double boiler, mix together the egg yolks and sugar. Add the hot milk and vanilla extract. Cook until the cream sticks to the back of a wooden spoon, stirring constantly.

Serve with crème anglaise.

PEAR AND PECAN FLAN

6 SERVINGS

Preparation Time: 15 minutes

Cooking Time: 45 minutes

5	slices of bread
14 oz	(396 ml) can of halved pears
1/2 cup	(50 ml) chopped pecans
2 cups	(500 ml) milk
1/2 tsp	(2 ml) vanilla extract
1/2 cup	(50 ml) sugar
1 tsp	(5 ml) baking powder
3	medium eggs
2 tbsp	(25 ml) icing sugar
6	sprigs of fresh mint (optional)

Preheat the oven to 350°F (180°C). Lightly toast the slices of bread and place them in a lightly greased 9 in (23 cm) pie plate.

Slice the pears, and garnish the slices of bread with pears and pecans.

In a saucepan warm the milk, being careful that it does not boil. Add the vanilla extract, sugar and baking powder. Mix well and remove from heat.

Incorporate the eggs to the mixture and pour over the pears. Bake for 40 to 45 minutes.

Let cool. When serving, sprinkle with icing sugar and garnish with fresh mint leaves.

LEMON LIME PIE

12 SERVINGS

Preparation Time: 30 minutes
Cooking Time: 30 minutes

1	pie dough
	beans or dried peas, in sufficient quantity (optional)
3	lemons
3	limes
3	medium eggs
1/4 cup	(50 ml) sugar
1/2 cup	(125 ml) milk
1 tbsp	(15 ml) butter
1 tbsp	(15 ml) cornstarch
1 tbsp	(15 ml) all-purpose flour
2 tbsp	(25 ml) plain yogurt
2 tbsp	(25 ml) icing sugar
4	sprigs of lemon grass

Preheat the oven to 350°F (180°C). Line a quiche mold or a 10 in (25 cm) pie pan with the dough. Fill with dried peas or beans, or prick the bottom of the pastry shell with a fork. Bake for 15 to 20 minutes (remove peas) and let set.

Remove the zest from the 2 lemons and 2 limes (keep a bit of zest for garnishing) and cut into thin strips. Place the zests in a saucepan with the juice of the 2 lemons and 2 limes. Add the eggs, sugar, milk and butter. Mix and cook over low heat.

Dilute the cornstarch and flour in a bit of water. Pour into the saucepan and thicken the lemon cream. When the lemon cream is thick, remove the saucepan from the stove and add the yogurt. Mix well.

Garnish the bottom of the pie with the lemon cream and sprinkle with icing sugar. Place in the oven under the broiler for a few minutes.

Garnish the top with lemon and lime slices, and zests. Serve warm or cold.

CHEESE AND PEAR PIE

8 TO 10 SERVINGS

Preparation Time: 15 minutes
Cooking Time: 50 minutes

12 oz	(341 ml) beer
1/2 cup	(125 ml) sugar
4	eggs
3/4 cup	(175 ml) all-purpose flour
1	pinch of salt
3/4 cup	(175 ml) milk
1 tsp	(5 ml) vanilla extract
1 cup	(250 ml) Havarti cheese
19 oz	(540 ml) can of pears, drained and cut in half

In a pan, bring the beer and sugar to a boil and reduce by 75%. Set aside and let cool.

Preheat the oven to 375°F (190°C). In a bowl, mix together the eggs, beer, flour, salt, milk, vanilla and cheese. Mix well.

Pour into a greased 9 in (23 cm) pie plate. Garnish with pears and bake for approximately 40 to 45 minutes.

CHOCOLATE PIE WITH RASPBERRY CREAM

8 SERVINGS

Preparation Time: 30 minutes
Refrigeration Time: 3 hours

CHOCOLATE CHIP PIE CRUST

1 1/3 cups	(325 ml)	all-purpose flour
2 tbsp	(25 ml)	sugar
1		pinch of salt
1/2 cup	(125 ml)	butter, cut into pieces
1/2 cup	(125 ml)	chocolate chips
4 tbsp	(60 ml)	ice water

CHOCOLATE FILLING

1/2 lb	(250 g)	semi-sweet chocolate
2 tbsp	(25 ml)	soft butter
2		medium eggs
1/2 cup	(125 ml)	35% cream, whipped

RASPBERRY MOUSSE

1 lb 2 oz	(300 g)	frozen raspberries, thawed
1/2 cup	(125 ml)	sugar
1/4 cup	(50 ml)	water
1/4 cup	(50 ml)	raspberry cream
1 1/2		packages of unflavored gelatin
1/2 cup	(125 ml)	35% cream, whipped

GARNISH

	fresh fruit, of choice
8	sprigs of fresh mint

PIE CRUST

Preheat the oven to 350°F (180°C). In a food processor, combine the flour, sugar and salt and mix for 15 to 20 seconds until smooth. Add the butter and mix for another 15 to 20 seconds. Add the chocolate chips and mix for approximately 10 seconds. Incorporate the ice water and mix until the dough detaches from the sides of the bowl.

Remove from the bowl and shape into a ball. Refrigerate for 30 minutes.

On a floured surface, roll out the dough into a 12 in (30 cm) circle. Place the dough in a glass pie plate. Cover with a sheet of wax paper or aluminum paper. Fill with dried beans or pie weights and bake for 20 minutes. Remove the beans and the paper, and continue to bake for 10 minutes. Set aside and let cool.

CHOCOLATE FILLING

In a double boiler or saucepan, melt the chocolate and butter over very low heat. Remove from the stove and add the eggs.

Cool in the refrigerator for 5 minutes and add the whipped cream. Mix well and pour into the chocolate chip crust. Place in the refrigerator for 30 minutes.

RASPBERRY MOUSSE

In a saucepan, cook the raspberries, sugar, water and raspberry cream over low heat for 2 minutes. Mix in the gelatin.

With a food processor, reduce the raspberry preparation to a purée, strain and cool in the refrigerator until it begins to set.

Add the whipped cream, mix and pour over the chocolate filling. Refrigerate for 2 hours. Garnish with fresh fruit and mint.

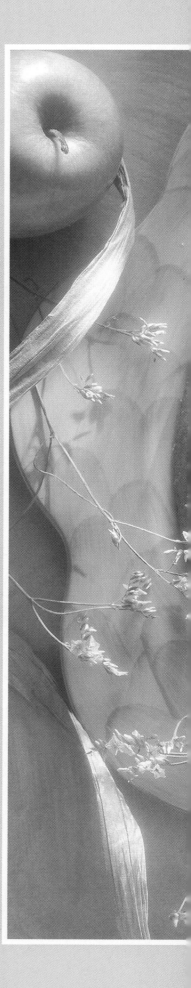

TATIN MAPLE PIE

6 SERVINGS

Preparation Time: 20 minutes
Cooking Time: 30 minutes

PIE

2 tbsp	(25 ml) butter
6	apples, peeled, cored, and cut in cubes
3/4 cup	(175 ml) maple syrup
1	pie dough, rolled out

MAPLE CRÈME ANGLAISE (optional)

4	medium egg yolks
1/2 cup	(125 ml) maple syrup (optional)
1 1/2 cups	(375 ml) warm milk
1/2 tsp	(2 ml) cornstarch, diluted in a small amount of water

GARNISH

fresh mint leaves
fresh berries, of choice

PIE

Preheat the oven to 350°F (180°C). In a saucepan, melt the butter and sauté the apples. Add the maple syrup and caramelize.

Pour the mixture into a pie pan, and cover with the pie dough. Bake for 15 to 20 minutes.

Remove from the oven and let stand for 5 minutes. Remove from the pie plate by turning upside down.

MAPLE CRÈME ANGLAISE

In a double boiler or in a saucepan, mix together the egg yolks and maple syrup. Cook over low heat. Add the hot milk and corn syrup. Cook until the cream sticks to the back of a wooden spoon. Pour into a large bowl and cool.

Serve the pie on a plate lined with the crème anglaise. Garnish with mint leaves and berries.

CARAMELIZED PEACH PIE

10 SERVINGS
Preparation Time: 20 minutes
Cooking Time: 45 minutes

SPONGE CAKE
2	eggs
2	egg yolks
3/4 cup	(175 ml) sugar
3/4 cup	(175 ml) butter
3/4 cup	(175 ml) flour
1/3 cup	(75 ml) potato starch or cornstarch
1	pinch of salt
1 tsp	(5 ml) vanilla extract
3/4 cup	(175 ml) almond powder
2	egg whites, whipped to form soft peaks

TOPPING
2 cups	(500 ml) cranberries
1 cup	(250 ml) cranberry juice
3/4 cup	(175 ml) sugar
1/2	small package of unflavored gelatin, set in 2 tbsp (25 ml) of cold water

PEACH GARNISH
1 tbsp	(15 ml) butter
5 to 6	peaches, peeled, pitted, and thinly sliced

SPONGE CAKE

Preheat the oven to 350°F (180°C). In a bowl, combine the eggs, egg yolks and sugar. Mix with an electric mixer until the mixture whitens.

Slowly add the butter, flour, starch, salt and vanilla. Fold in the almond powder and whipped egg whites. Pour into a greased, and floured 9 in (23 cm) pie pan. Bake for 25 to 30 minutes. Let cool.

TOPPING

In a saucepan, combine the cranberries, cranberry juice, sugar and gelatin and bring to a boil. Mix well and let simmer for 5 minutes over low heat. Purée in a food processor, strain and pour 3/4 of the mixture over the sponge cake.

PEACH GARNISH

In a saucepan, melt the butter and caramelize the peaches and the remaining cranberry topping. Place on top of the sponge cake.

CAPPUCCINO PIE

8 TO 10 SERVINGS

Preparation Time: 25 minutes

Cooking Time: 40 minutes

1	pie crust, cooked and cooled
1/4 cup	(50 ml) coffee liqueur (Kahlua)
1 tbsp	(15 ml) instant espresso coffee granules
8 oz	package of cream cheese, softened
14 oz	can of sweet condensed milk
2	eggs, beaten
2 tbsp	(25 ml) cocoa powder
GARNISH	
1 cup	(250 ml) 35% cream, whipped

Preheat the oven to 325°F (180°C). In a small bowl, mix together Kahlua and instant espresso coffee granules until the granules dissolve.

In another large bowl, whip together the cheese and the condensed milk. Add the eggs, liqueur mixture and cocoa. Mix well.

Pour into the pie crust and bake for 40 minutes. Let cool, refrigerate, and serve with whip cream.

CHOCOLATE AND GRAPE TARTS

4 SERVINGS

Preparation Time: 15 minutes

Cooking Time: 20 minutes

1/2 lb	(250 g) pie dough
40	purple grapes
1/3 cup	(75 ml) apricot jelly
2 tbsp	(25 ml) water
CHOCOLATE FILLING	
1/2 cup	(125 ml) 35% cream
4 oz	(125 g) semi-sweet chocolate
2 tbsp	(25 ml) butter

Preheat the oven to 350°F (180°C). On a floured surface, roll out the dough and cut into 4 circles, big enough to cover the bottom of 4 aluminum tart molds. Prick the entire bottom of the dough with a fork and bake for 10 to 12 minutes.

CHOCOLATE FILLING

In a saucepan, bring the cream to a boil and remove from heat. Add the chocolate and butter. Whisk until the chocolate has melted completely; let cool. Then whip with an electric mixer for 2 to 3 minutes.

Pour the mixture into the tart molds and garnish with grapes; set aside.

In a small saucepan, combine the apricot jelly and water. Mix well and cook over low heat for 2 to 3 minutes. Pour the apricot jelly over the grapes and serve.

MAPLE SYRUP PIE

6 TO 8 SERVINGS

Preparation Time: 15 minutes

Cooking Time: 15 minutes

4 tbsp	(50 ml) butter
6 tbsp	(90 ml) flour
1 1/2 cups	(375 ml) maple syrup
1/2 cup	(125 ml) milk
1	pie crust, baked

In a saucepan, melt the butter over low heat. Add the flour and continue cooking for 1 minute; mixing well. Remove from the stove and add the maple syrup and milk.

Put back on the stove and let simmer over medium heat until thick. Pour the mixture into the pie crust and let cool before serving.

CHOCOLATE TARTS WITH BERRIES

8 SERVINGS

Preparation Time: 40 minutes
Refrigeration Time: 1 hour

CRÈME ANGLAISE WITH BEER

4	egg yolks
1/2 cup	(125 ml) sugar
3/4 cup	(175 ml) hot milk
1 tsp	(5 ml) cornstarch
3/4 cup	(175 ml) beer, hot
1 tsp	(5 ml) vanilla extract

BERRIES SOAKED IN GINGER AND GREEN PEPPERCORNS

3/4 cup	(175 ml) beer
2 cups	(500 ml) fresh berries, of choice
1/4 cup	(50 ml) sugar
1/2 tsp	(2 ml) ground ginger
1/2 tsp	(2 ml) green peppercorns

GARNISH

4 to 6	chocolate cups
	mint leaves

CRÈME ANGLAISE WITH BEER

In a double boiler or a small saucepan, mix together the egg yolks and sugar and cook over very low heat. Add the hot milk, cornstarch, beer and vanilla. Cook until the cream sticks to the back of a wooden spoon, stirring constantly. Pour into a bowl, let cool and set aside.

BERRIES SOAKED IN GINGER AND GREEN PEPPERCORNS

In a saucepan, reduce the beer by half and let cool. Place the berries in a bowl, pour the reduced beer over the berries, and sprinkle with sugar, ginger and green peppercorns. Let soak for an hour in the refrigerator. Add the Crème Anglaise and mix. Serve in the chocolate cups and garnish with mint leaves.

GLAZED BERRY TARTS

6 SERVINGS

Preparation Time: 15 minutes
Cooking Time: 10 minutes

RASPBERRY COULIS

1 cup	(250 ml) raspberries, fresh or frozen
2 tbsp	(25 ml) apple juice
1 tsp	(5 ml) lemon juice
2 tbsp	(25 ml) granulated sugar
14 oz	(398 ml) can of sliced peaches (keep the juice)
1/2 cup	(125 ml) fresh strawberries
1/2 cup	(125 ml) fresh raspberries
1/2 cup	(125 ml) fresh blueberries
1/2 cup	(125 ml) fresh cherries, pitted
6	small cakes, tart shape
6	scoops of vanilla ice cream

RASPBERRY COULIS

In a saucepan, mix together the ingredients of the coulis, and simmer for 5 minutes. Strain and return to the saucepan; set aside.

Add the peach juice and the berries to the raspberry coulis. Cook over low heat and let simmer for 3 minutes (if necessary thicken with a little cornstarch, diluted in water).

Garnish the small cakes with vanilla ice cream and cover with the berry sauce.

RASPBERRY BANANA CREAM PIE

6 TO 8 SERVINGS

Preparation Time: 20 minutes
Cooking Time: 45 minutes

1	pie dough, rolled out
1 cup	(250 ml) raspberries, fresh or frozen
1	banana, cut into rounds
4	medium eggs
1/2 cup	(125 ml) sugar
1/2 cup	(125 ml) almond powder
2 tbsp	(25 ml) melted butter
1 cup	(250 ml) hot milk
1 tsp	(5 ml) vanilla extract
2 tbsp	(25 ml) banana cream
1/2 cup	(125 ml) all-purpose flour
1 tbsp	(15 ml) icing sugar

Preheat the oven to 300°F (150°C). Place the dough in a 9 in (23 cm) pie plate and fill with raspberries and banana; set aside.

In a bowl, mix together the eggs, sugar, almond powder and butter. Add the milk, vanilla, banana cream and flour; mix well.

Pour the mixture into the pie plate and bake for approximately 45 minutes. Let cool and sprinkle with icing sugar before serving.

BLUEBERRY ALMOND PIE

8 SERVINGS

Preparation Time: 15 minutes
Cooking Time: 40 minutes

1	pie dough, rolled out
2	medium eggs
1 cup	(250 ml) icing sugar or 1/2 cup (125 ml) sugar
1/3 cup	(75 ml) butter, softened
2 tbsp	(25 ml) all-purpose flour
3/4 cup	(175 ml) almond powder
2 cups	(500 ml) blueberries, fresh or frozen
1 tbsp	(15 ml) icing sugar

Preheat the oven to 350°F (180°C). Place the dough in a 9 in (23 cm) pie plate; let set in the fridge.

With a food processor or an electric mixer, mix together the eggs, icing sugar, butter, flour and almond powder.

Pour the mixture into the pie shell. Cover with blueberries and bake for 35 to 40 minutes. Let cool and sprinkle with icing sugar.

HEALTHY PEACH PIE

10 TO 12 SERVINGS

Preparation Time: 10 minutes
Cooking Time: 45 minutes

5	slices of bread
3	medium eggs
2 cups	(500 ml) milk
28 oz	(798 ml) can of peaches, halved, and drained (keep the syrup)
1/4 cup	(50 ml) honey
3/4 cup	(175 ml) ricotta cheese
1 tsp	(5 ml) vanilla extract
1/2 cup	(125 ml) rolled oats

GARNISH

fresh fruit of choice

Preheat the oven to 350°F (180 °C). On a flat surface, flatten the bread slices using a rolling pin and place them in a 9 to 10 in (23 to 25 cm) greased, ceramic pie pan. Bake for 5 minutes, set aside.

With a food processor, or an electric mixer, combine the eggs, milk, peach syrup, honey, ricotta cheese, vanilla and rolled oats; set aside.

Fill the bread shell with the peaches and pour the egg mixture over the peaches. Bake for approximately 35 to 45 minutes.

APPLE AND MIXED FRUIT PIE

8 TO 10 SERVINGS

Preparation Time: 15 minutes
Cooking Time: 45 minutes

1	pie dough, rolled out
2 cups	(500 ml) apple sauce
1 1/2 cups	(375 ml) preserved fruits, cut into pieces
2	medium eggs
1 1/2 cups	(375 ml) milk
1/3 cup	(75 ml) sugar
1/3 cup	(75 ml) almond powder
1 tsp	(5 ml) vanilla extract
1 tbsp	(15 ml) cornstarch, diluted in water
	ground nutmeg, to taste
2	apples, peeled, cored and sliced

GARNISH

1/2 cup	(125 ml) oatmeal
1/4 cup	(50 ml) brown sugar
2 tbsp	(25 ml) softened butter

Preheat the oven to 350°F (180°C). Place the dough in a 9 in (23 cm) pie plate, or a deep aluminum pie plate.

Fill with apple sauce and preserved fruits; set aside. In a bowl, mix together the eggs, milk, sugar, almond powder, vanilla extract and cornstarch. Pour the egg mixture into the pie plate.

Garnish with apple slices and sprinkle with nutmeg. In a bowl, mix together the oatmeal, brown sugar and butter. Place the mixture on top of the apples and bake for approximately 45 minutes.

ICE CREAM DELIGHT

4 SERVINGS

Preparation Time: 20 minutes

Cooking Time: 5 minutes

2 cups (500 ml) chocolate chip ice cream

CRÊPE BATTER
  1 egg
3/4 cup (175 ml) all-purpose flour
  2 tsp (10 ml) icing sugar
  1 cup (250 ml) milk
1 tbsp (15 ml) melted butter
      vanilla extract, to taste
  1 pinch of salt
2 tbsp (25 ml) corn oil

In a bowl, mix together all the ingredients of the crêpe batter, except the oil.

In a non-stick frying pan, heat the oil and cook the crêpes over medium heat. Make sure to spread the mixture well, so as to obtain thin crêpes. Let cool.

Place ice cream in the middle of the crêpes and roll. Keep in the freezer until ready to serve.

FRUITY BREAD ROLLS WITH CHOCOLATE SAUCE

4 SERVINGS

Preparation Time: 15 minutes

Cooking Time: 20 minutes

  4 eggs
1 cup (250 ml) milk
1/3 cup (75 ml) icing sugar
2 tbsp (25 ml) honey
  8 slices of bread
      fresh fruit of choice, diced
1 tbsp (15 ml) icing sugar
1 cup (250 ml) chocolate sauce

Preheat the oven to 350°F (180°C). In a bowl, combine the eggs, milk, icing sugar and honey and mix well; set aside.

On a countertop, lightly flatten the bread slices, fill them with fresh fruit and roll up. Dip the rolls into the egg mixture and place in a greased, ovenproof dish. Bake for 15 to 20 minutes.

Sprinkle with icing sugar and serve on a bed of chocolate sauce.

CHOCOLATE WAFFLES

4 SERVINGS

Preparation Time: 25 minutes
Cooking Time: 6 minutes

2 cups (500 ml) whole wheat flour
1/3 cup (75 ml) cocoa powder, sifted
1/2 cup (125 ml) sugar
1/2 tsp (2 ml) ground cinnamon
2 tsp (10 ml) baking powder
1/2 tsp (2 ml) salt
1 cup (250 ml) milk
2 tbsp (25 ml) corn oil
2 tbsp (25 ml) creamy peanut butter
1 tsp (5 ml) vanilla extract
3 medium egg whites,
lightly whipped

In a bowl, combine the flour, cocoa, sugar, cinnamon, baking powder and salt.

Incorporate the milk, corn oil, peanut butter and vanilla extract; mix until the mixture is smooth.

Slowly incorporate the whipped egg whites.

Heat a waffle iron, lightly sprayed with cooking spray. Pour the dough in the middle of the preheated waffle iron and cook for approximately 6 minutes or until the waffle is crispy. Repeat the procedure and keep the waffles warm in the oven at 250°F (120°C), covered with aluminum foil.

APPLE CRÊPES WITH MAPLE SAUCE

4 SERVINGS

Preparation Time: 20 minutes
Cooking Time: 30 minutes

CRÊPE BATTER
1 cup (250 ml) all-purpose flour
2 medium eggs
1 1/2 cup (375 ml) milk
1 tsp (5 ml) orange zest
1 tsp (5 ml) lemon zest
2 tbsp (25 ml) corn oil

APPLE FILLING
1/4 cup (50 ml) butter
1/3 cup (75 ml) sugar
6 apples, peeled, cored and sliced

SAUCE
1 cup (250 ml) sugar
1/4 cup (50 ml) water
3/4 cup (175 ml) 35% cream
1/2 cup (125 ml) maple syrup

CRÊPES

In a bowl or in a food processor, mix together the flour and eggs. Add the milk and mix until the mixture is smooth. Add the zest and let set for 1 hour. Cook eight, 10 in (25 cm) crêpes in a hot, non-stick pan with a little heated oil; set aside.

APPLE FILLING

In a frying pan, melt the butter and slowly increase the heat. Add the sugar and cook for approximately 5 minutes until golden. Add the apples and cook over low heat for 10 minutes. Remove from the stove and set aside.

SAUCE

In a saucepan, combine the sugar and water; cook until the syrup is a golden color. Reduce the heat and slowly add the cream. Add the maple syrup and simmer for 5 minutes. Remove from the stove.

Pour the apple filling over the 8 crêpes, roll them up and place them on plates. Garnish the crêpes with maple sauce and serve.

CRÊPES WITH GLAZED BERRIES AND RASPBERRY CREAM

4 SERVINGS
Preparation Time: 30 minutes
Cooking Time: 30 minutes

1/2 cup	(125 ml)	35% cream, whipped
3/4 cup	(175 ml)	fresh strawberries
3/4 cup	(175 ml)	fresh raspberries
3/4 cup	(175 ml)	fresh blueberries

GARNISH

4		clusters fresh mint

CRÊPE BATTER

1		medium egg
1 cup	(250 ml)	milk
3/4 cup	(175 ml)	all-purpose flour
2 tsp	(10 ml)	icing sugar
1		pinch of salt
1 tbsp	(15 ml)	corn oil

CRÈME ANGLAISE

4		medium egg yolks
1/4 cup	(50 ml)	honey
1 1/2 cups	(375 ml)	warm milk
1 tsp	(5 ml)	vanilla extract
1/4 cup	(50 ml)	raspberry cream

CRÊPES

In a bowl, mix together all the crêpe ingredients, with the exception of the oil. In a non-stick pan, heat the oil and cook the crêpes over medium heat. Let cool and set aside.

CRÈME ANGLAISE

In a double boiler, combine the egg yolks and the honey. Add the warm milk, vanilla extract and the raspberry cream. Heat and stir constantly until the cream sticks to the back of a wooden spoon. Let cool and gently mix with the whipped cream.

In a bowl, mix together the small berries, being careful not to crush them and stuff the crêpes with this filling. Place the crêpes in an ovenproof dish and cover with cream. Brown in the oven under the broiler for a few seconds. Garnish with mint leaves and serve.

ORANGE PUDDING

8 TO 10 SERVINGS
Preparation Time: 15 minutes
Cooking Time: 1 hour

4	medium eggs
1 cup	(250 ml) milk
3/4 cup	(175 ml) sugar
1 tbsp	(15 ml) vanilla extract
2	bananas, peeled and mashed
1/4 tsp	(2 ml) ground cinnamon
14 oz	(398 ml) fruit salad
8	slices of bread, cut into strips
1/4 cup	(50 ml) chopped walnuts
	zest of 1 orange
	zest of 1 lemon
1/4 cup	(50 ml) raisins
	grated coconut (optional)

Preheat the oven to 350°F (180°C). In a large bowl, combine the eggs, milk, sugar, vanilla extract, bananas and cinnamon; mix well.

Add the fruit salad, bread strips, walnuts, zests and raisins. Mix delicately with a spatula or spoon.

Pour into a greased loaf pan, and bake for approximately 1 hour. Garnish with grated coconut if desired.

BLACK CHERRY PUDDING

4 SERVINGS
Preparation Time: 15 minutes
Cooking Time: 45 minutes

4	eggs
1 cup	(250 ml) milk
3/4 cup	(175 ml) all-purpose flour
3/4 cup	(175 ml) sugar
1 tsp	(5 ml) vanilla extract
4	slices of white bread, cut into pieces
14 oz	(398 ml) black cherries, pitted and cut into pieces
1/3 cup	(75 ml) apple jelly, melted with 2 tbsp (25 ml) water

Preheat the oven to 350°F (180°C). In a bowl, combine the eggs, milk, flour and vanilla; mix well and set aside.

Place the bread pieces on the bottom of a greased 9 in (23 cm) pie plate or deep ceramic pie pan. Fill with the black cherries. Cover with the egg mixture and bake in the oven for 40 to 45 minutes. Let cool and garnish with melted apple jelly.

MYSTERY BREAD PUDDING

6 TO 8 SERVINGS

Preparation Time: 20 minutes
Cooking Time: 1 hour

4		medium egg yolks
1/2 cup	(125 ml)	sugar
3/4 cup	(175 ml)	cocoa powder
2 tbsp	(25 ml)	molasses
2 tbsp	(25 ml)	creamy peanut butter
1 cup	(250 ml)	mashed bananas
1 1/2 cups	(375 ml)	milk
6 cups	(1.5 L)	white bread, cut into pieces
1/3 cup	(75 ml)	raisins
1 tsp	(5 ml)	ground cinnamon
1 tsp	(5 ml)	vanilla extract
4		medium egg whites

SAUCE

2 tbsp	(25 ml)	butter
1/2 cup	(125 ml)	dark brown sugar
1/4 cup	(50 ml)	brown rum (optional)
1 tbsp	(15 ml)	cornstarch
1 1/4 cups	(300 ml)	milk
1 tsp	(5 ml)	vanilla extract

Preheat the oven to 325°F (160°C) and grease a square 8 in (20 cm) cake pan. In a bowl, mix together the egg yolks and the sugar. Mix until the mixture whitens. Add the cocoa powder, molasses, peanut butter, bananas and milk; mix well.

Add the bread pieces, raisins, cinnamon and vanilla extract. Beat the egg whites to form soft peaks and then add to the bread pudding.

Place the mixture in the pan and bake for 1 hour, or until a knife comes out clean when inserted into the middle of the pudding.

SAUCE

In a saucepan, melt the butter over medium heat and add the brown sugar. Add the rum and cook for 1 hour, stirring constantly. Dilute the cornstarch in the milk and add to the saucepan. Bring to a boil, stirring continuously and remove from the stove. Add the vanilla extract.

Serve the pudding warm, with hot rum sauce.

PINEAPPLE AND RAISIN CRISP

8 SERVINGS

Preparation Time: 15 minutes
Cooking Time: 35 minutes

2 cups	(500 ml)	canned pineapples, cut into cubes, with a little juice
1/3 cup	(75 ml)	raisins
1/3 cup	(75 ml)	sugar
1/2 cup	(125 ml)	all-purpose flour
2		muffins, crumbled
1/2 cup	(125 ml)	rolled oats
1/2 cup	(125 ml)	brown sugar
1		pinch of cinnamon
1		pinch of nutmeg
1		pinch of salt
3/4 cup	(175 ml)	butter

Preheat the oven to 350°F (180°C). Place the pineapples and the raisins in a buttered Pyrex dish. Sprinkle with sugar and set aside.

In a bowl, combine the flour, rolled oats, muffins, brown sugar, cinnamon, nutmeg, salt and butter. Garnish the pineapples with this preparation and bake for approximately 30 to 35 minutes.

WHOLE WHEAT BANANA BREAD AND HONEY TERRINE

8 TO 10 SERVINGS
Preparation Time: 20 minutes
Cooking Time: 1 hour 15 minutes

TERRINE
1	medium egg
1 cup	(250 ml) milk
2 tbsp	(25 ml) honey
1 tsp	(5 ml) butter
4	slices of bread
4	medium eggs
2 cups	(500 ml) milk
2 tbsp	(25 ml) cornstarch
1/4 cup	(50 ml) honey
2	bananas, sliced
1/4 cup	(50 ml) raisins
1	package of unflavored gelatin
2 tbsp	(25 ml) cold water
1/4 cup	(50 ml) warm water

STRAWBERRY COULIS
10 oz	(300 g) frozen strawberries (thawed)
3/4 cup	(175 ml) unsweetened apple juice
1/4 cup	(50 ml) honey

GARNISH
fresh fruit of choice

TERRINE

Preheat the oven to 300°F (150°C). In a bowl, mix together the eggs, milk and honey. Soak the bread slices in this mixture. In a pan, melt the butter over medium heat, and cook the bread for 1 minute, on each side, until golden. Cover the bottom of a lightly greased terrine mold with the bread slices; set aside.

In a bowl, combine the eggs, milk, cornstarch, honey, bananas and raisins. Incorporate the gelatin, which has set in cold water and has been diluted with warm water. Pour into the terrine and bake for approximately 1 hour to 1 hour 15 minutes; refrigerate.

STRAWBERRY COULIS

In a saucepan, bring the strawberries, apple juice, and honey to a boil. Purée in a food processor and strain.

Remove the terrine from the mold and slice. Serve with strawberry coulis and garnish with fresh fruit.

TABLE OF CONTENTS